MERSEY SHIPPING
The Twilight Years

MERSEY SHIPPING
The Twilight Years

Ian Collard

TEMPUS

First published 2000
Reprinted 2003
Copyright © Ian Collard, 2000

Tempus Publishing Limited
The Mill, Brimscombe Port,
Stroud, Gloucestershire, GL5 2QG

ISBN 0 7524 1732 0

Typesetting and origination by
Tempus Publishing Limited
Printed in Great Britain by
Midway Colour Print, Wiltshire

Contents

Acknowledgements

I wish to thank the staff at the Mersey Docks and Harbour Company for all the help and assistance they gave me in the preparation of the work. I also wish to thank Louis Sampson who processed and developed most of the films that provided the basis for this book.

Introduction

Photographs can capture the mood and spirit of an occasion and provide a frozen image of a moment in time that can never be repeated. Some become a permanent record of an event in history such as the assassination of an American president, or the coronation of a British King or Queen. Many, however, are taken by ordinary people of everyday events, like births, christenings, weddings or other celebrations.

When I took the photographs contained in this book I never imagined the dramatic effect they would have on me when I had them processed several decades later. The majority of the images were taken in the 1960s, although I had the films printed only recently.

Seeing the pictures was like stepping into a time machine and being transported back to a different age. As we are only talking about a period of thirty years this may sound a little dramatic, but they illustrated how the world changes so quickly and life moves on before we have time to relish the moment.

Most of the photographs were taken on the eve of a revolution in the shipping industry which had not been predicted but came about suddenly, changing everything virtually overnight. Containerization caused the demise of some shipping lines which had been in business for over a hundred years. Stevedores, hauliers, ship-repairers and many other ancillary businesses were affected, and this had an important knock-on effect on the local economy in areas of the country that relied on international maritime trade.

On Merseyside, the Mersey Docks and Harbour Company was forced to rationalize its operations by closing down the whole of the South Docks system and investing in a new container system at the Royal Seaforth Dock. The passenger liners were finding it increasingly difficult to compete with the airlines, and, by the middle of the 1960s most were either sold or transferred to southern ports to experiment in the cruising trade. The Princes Landing Stage was demolished and replaced by a smaller, more compact structure, which provided berths for the Mersey Ferries and the ships of the Isle of Man Steam Packet.

In 1971 the Mersey Docks and Harbour Company owned and controlled the docks at Liverpool and Birkenhead. They acted as the Pilotage Authority, Lighthouse and Harbour Authority. Their jurisdiction had a landward limit one and a half miles above the Manchester Ship Canal and the seaward limit covered a large part of the Irish Sea, Anglesey to the Calf of Man and Ayre Point, and up to St Bees Head, Cumbria. The Port Authority had pilot boats stationed at the Mersey Bar and Port Lynas, off the coast of Anglesey, and the service was provided by approximately 180 self-employed and highly qualified personnel.

As the tidal range in the River Mersey precludes cargo handling in the river, such operations are carried out from floating landing stages. The Princess and George's Landing Stages formed a continuous structure 2,534ft long by 80ft wide. Woodside Stage was used by the Mersey ferries and cattle boats, and the Tranmere Terminal was for the discharge of crude oil.

The Docks extend eight miles at Liverpool and four and a half miles at Birkenhead. Liverpool has thirty miles of quays, Birkenhead a further ten. The total area of responsibility of the Company was 2,580 acres, with a total water area of 730 acres. In 1971 there were 188 foreign berths, forty coastwise and the total area of transit sheds was over one million square yards. There were 140 miles of rail facilities, dredging was carried out by four self-propelled grab-hopper dredgers and survey and salvage operations were performed by vessels owned by the company. 14,320 vessels used the Port with the total cargo handled amounting to 29,906,000 tons.

I am glad that I was there to record a period of time that had both maritime and local significance. The book is a record of how time moves on and how things that we regard as everyday items in our lives quickly change and disappear. We are able to capture and preserve time for future generations to view, allowing them to make judgements on events in history. If we are to move forward it is important that we are able to revisit the past and taste, evaluate and appreciate days gone by.

I hope that the photographs evoke memories and remind you of our rich maritime past, and that they give you as much pleasure and enjoyment as they have given me while I have been researching and compiling the material. The book has illustrated a period of great change in the shipping industry and the fortunes of one of the most important employers on Merseyside. However nostalgic it may be, it is also a story of success, as the Dock Company has survived to become one of the most thriving companies in the country.

One

The Liners

Liverpool was a significant port for a number of major shipping lines in this period. Cunard's main headquarters was located at the Pier Head, as they maintained a regular passenger and freight liner service to New York, Quebec and Montreal.

Canadian Pacific Steamships' three 'Empress' ships sailed to Canada and Elder Dempster's passenger vessels *Aureol*, *Apapa* and *Accra* carried mail, passengers and cargo to West African ports. Passengers were able to sail to Karachi and Bombay by Anchor Line and to Barbados, Trinidad and Brazilian ports by the Booth Line. The *Reina Del Mar* of the Pacific Steam Navigation Company also provided a passenger link with South American ports, until she was converted to a cruise liner in 1963.

The large passenger liners normally used the Princes Landing Stage as their point of arrival or departure, because of its central location and railway station with links to the capital.

Empress of England (957/25,585grt) on an early morning arrival at Princes Landing Stage from Montreal.

Northern Stars berths at Liverpool Landing Stage following her trial and delivery to her owners in 1962. She then proceeded to Southampton where she sailed on her maiden voyage on 10 July with over 1400 passengers and 480 crew on board. With her sister *Southern Cross*, she completed many round-the-world voyages until she was withdrawn from service in 1975. Still relatively young, she arrived at the ship breakers in Taiwan on 11 December that year for demolition.

Kungsholm, 1966, of the Swedish America Line, 26,678grt, 201m x 26m. Built at John Brown's in Clydebank, she was capable of 22 knots. *Kungsholm* was operated on the Gothenburg, Copenhagen to New York transatlantic service for Swedish America Line, as well as world cruises, until she was sold to P&O in 1979 when she was renamed *Sea Princess*. Operated by the Princess Cruises division of P&O, she was again renamed *Victoria* in 1995 and was sold in 2002 becoming *Mona Lisa*.

Reina Del Mar (1956/20747grt) prepares to sail from Princes Landing Stage on a Travel Saving cruise. She was built in 1956 for the Pacific Steam Navigation Company. She was chartered by the Travel Saving Association in 1963 and converted to a cruise liner in 1964. She was broken up in Kaohsuing, Taiwan, in 1975.

Kungsholm is shown here diverted to Liverpool, because of bad weather in the Irish Sea, from her call at Llandudno, North Wales, while on a Round Britain cruise. *Empress of Canada* (1961/27,284grt) is also at Princes Landing Stage.

Arkadia, 1931, Greek Line, 20,648grt, 180m x 26m, 19½knots. She was originally built as the three-funnelled *Monarch of Bermuda* by Vickers at Barrow for the Furness Line's New York to Bermuda route. Following a serious fire in 1947, she was converted to an emigrant carrier, operated by Shaw Savill, and renamed *New Australia*. In 1958 she was sold to the Greek Line and converted to a luxury passenger liner for their transatlantic service as well as for cruising. She was eventually sold and broken up in 1966.

Several information signs at Princes Landing Stage, direction motorists and passengers onto the liners, ferries and Irish Sea vessels, at the Pier Head.

Taxis queue at the Landing Stage to pick up passengers from a Canadian Pacific liner which had arrived earlier from Montreal.

The Cunard passenger liner *Mauretania* in Gladstone Graving Dock in November 1963 undertaking her annual overhaul. *Mauretania*, 35,677grt, was built by Cammell Laird in Birkenhead in 1939. She was 236m by 27m and had a service speed of 23 knots. She was broken up in Inverkeithing, Scotland, in 1965. Her earlier namesake was scrapped at the same yard.

Empress of Canada (1961 / 27,284grt) and *Empress of Britain* (1956 / 25,516grt) at the Canadian Pacific berth at Gladstone Dock. The two passenger liners were together for a short time each year prior to their annual overhaul. They would then leave the Port to undertake a series of winter cruises, returning the following year to resume the Canadian service.

Remuera, built 1948, New Zealand Shipping Company, 13,619grt, 162m x 21m, 17 knots. Originally the Cunard Line cargo-passenger vessel *Parhia*, sailing from Liverpool to New York. She was renamed *Remuera* in 1961 when she was sold to the New Zealand Shipping Company. She is seen here at Princes Landing Stage about to sail to London prior to her maiden voyage for the NZSC. She was renamed *Aramac* in 1965 and broken up at Kaohsiung in 1969.

Centaur visits Liverpool in 1964 on her delivery voyage from her builders, John Brown & Co. (Clydebank) Ltd. She was 8,262grt and 147m by 20m with a service speed of 20 knots. She was built for the Singapore to Fremantle service and was able to carry 190 passengers and 4,500 sheep. She was withdrawn from service in 1981 and was sold to China. In 1985 she was renamed *Hai Long* and, in 1986, *Hai Da*.

Aureol, 1951, Elder Dempster Line, 14,083grt, 164m x 21m, 16 knots. Flagship of the fleet and the largest of the liners to operate on the Liverpool to West Africa service. She took part in the Independence celebrations at Lagos, Nigeria, in 1960 and operated from Liverpool until she was transferred to Southampton in 1972. She was withdrawn in 1974, when she was sold and renamed *Marianna V1*.

Accra, 1947, Elder Dempster Line, 11,644grt, 144m x 20m, 16 knots. *Accra* sailed with passengers and cargo to West Africa with her sisters *Apapa* and *Aureol* until 1967, when she was withdrawn and broken up at Cartegena, Spain.

Southern Cross, 1955, Shaw Savill Line, 20,203grt, 184m x 24m, 20 knots. *Southern Cross* was the first British liner to have her funnel aft of the passenger decks. This allowed for long uninterrupted decks where passengers could play, relax and sunbathe. This view dates from 1971 while she was completing a number of cruises out of Liverpool for her original owners. She was sold in 1975 and renamed *Calypso*, becoming the *Azure Seas* in 1980 and then *Ocean Breeze* in 1991.

Uganda, 1952, British India SNC, 14,430grt, 165m x 22m, 18 knots. *Uganda* was initially employed on the London-East Africa route with her sister *Kenya* until 1967 when the service was closed. Following conversion, she commenced service as an educational cruise liner in 1968. She was requisitioned as a hospital ship following the invasion of the Falkland Islands in 1982 and saw service there until the end of hostilities. She returned with troops and was back in service later that year. From 1983 to 1985 she was again used as a troop carrier. In 1986 she was sold, renamed *Triton* and was broken up at Kaohsiung.

Devonia, 1939, Bristol India Line, 11,275grt, 158m x 19m, 16 knots. Built as the *Devonshire* for the Bibby Line, she completed war service as a troopship. In 1962 she was sold to the British India Line and used for educational school cruises, until she was sold to the shipbreakers in La Spezia in 1967.

Dunera, 1937, British India SNC, 12,620grt, 157m x 19m, 14 knots. She was used as a troopship in the early years of the Second World War and in 1944 was the Headquarters ship of the 7th Army for the invasion of the south of France. At the end of hostilities she spent many years as a troopship in various parts of the world. In 1961 she was converted to a schoolship and was broken up in 1967.

Nevasa, 1956, British India SNC, 20,746grt, 186m x 24m, 17 knots. Designed and built as a troopship, *Nevasa* continued in this service until 1962 when she was laid up at in the River Fal. She was converted to an educational cruise ship in 1964 and was sold for breaking up in Taiwan in 1975.

A view of the bridge of the *Empress of Canada* (1961/27,284grt) showing the lock gates at the Gladstone River Entrance, as well as New Brighton on the Wirral coast.

Empress of Canada, 1961, Canadian Pacific Line, 27,284grt, 198m x 27m, 21 knots. On her maiden voyage, on 24 April 1961, she sailed from Liverpool to Montrealand. She spent most of her Canadian Pacific career on this service in the summer while also cruising in the winter. She arrived at Liverpool on 23 November 1971, was sold to Carnival Cruise Line in 1972 and renamed *Mardi Gras*. In 1993 she became the *Olympic* and was renamed the *Star of Texas* in 1994 . She was again renamed *Apollon* in 1996 by Direct Cruises and returned to the Mersey for a series of cruises.

In 1970 the Canadian Pacific liner *Empress of England* (1957/25,585grt) was sold to the Shaw Savill line and was renamed *Ocean Monarch*. She is seen here being repainted in her new owner's colours in Gladstone Dock, Liverpool. *Ocean Monarch* remained in service until 1975, when she was sold for scrap to Taiwan.

Above and below: Sylvania (1957/21,989grt) spent most of her life with Cunard, painted with a black hull but was painted white for cruising in 1967. She was sold to the Sitmar Line in 1968 and was renamed *Fair Wind*. In 1988 she became the *Dawn Princess* for Princess Cruises. In 1994 she was sold and renamed *Albatros* in 1994.

Carinthia, 1956, Cunard Line, 21,947grt, 185m x 24m, 20 knots. In 1967 *Carinthia* made the last passenger sailing for Cunard on the Liverpool to Montreal route and returned to Southampton, where she was laid up until 31 January 1968, when she was sold to Sitmar Line and renamed *Fairland*. In 1971 she was renamed *Fairsea*. The Sitmar Line was bought by P&O in 1988 and she was renamed *Fair Princess*.

Franconia, 1955, Cunard Line, 22,636grt, 185m x 24m, 20 knots. Launched as the *Ivernia*, in 1963 she was given a green hull and renamed *Franconia*. In 1967 she became the last Cunard liner to teminate a passenger sailing at Liverpool. She was laid up in the River Fal, in 1972, with her sister-ship *Carmania* and was bought by the Russians in 1973 and renamed *Fedor Shalyapin*.

Caledonia, 1948, Anchor Line, 11,252grt, 154m x 20m, 16½ knots. *Caledonia* was sold in 1965 and became an accommodation vessel at Amsterdam. She was disposed of in 1970 when she was broken up in Hamburg.

Circassia, 1937, Anchor Line, 11,170grt, 154m x 20m, 16½ knots. The *Circassia* took the last passenger sailing from Glasgow and Liverpool to Bombay in 1966 and was then broken up in Spain.

Above and below: The Aznar Line's passenger vessels *Monte Arucas* (1956/4,691grt) and *Monte Anaga* (1959/6,813grt) maintained a regular cruise programme from Liverpool to Spain and the Canary Islands up to their withdrawal from service in 1975.

Ocean Monarch (1951/13,581grt) in Cammel Laird's graving dock undertaking her annual overhaul. She was owned by Furness Lines and normally operated cruises from New York to Bermuda and Nassau. She was sold to the Bulgarian State Tourist Company in 1967 and renamed *Varna*. In 1977 she was renamed *Venus* by new Greek owners and in 1978 she became the *Reina Del Mar*. During a refit at Piraeus in 1981, she was destroyed by fire.

Passengers board the Canadian Pacific liner *Empress of Canada* (1961/27,284grt) in Gladstone Dock in 1968, as she prepares to sail to Canada.

A pipe band serenades passengers as their cruise liner departs from Liverpool in 1963 for a Mediterranean cruise.

The Isle of Man vessel *Manx Maid* (1962/2,724grt) moves slowly astern in the river, leaving the Cunard liner *Carinthia* (1956/21,947grt) and her tugs at Princes Landing Stage.

Empress of Britain, 1956, Canadian Pacific Line, 25,516grt, 195m x 26m, 21 knots. Launched by HM the Queen on 22 June 1955, she sailed on her maiden voyage from Liverpool on 20 April 1956 to Canada. She was also employed as a cruise liner and made her first cruise from Liverpool on 13 February 1962. In 1964 she was sold to the Greek Line to be the *Queen Anna Maria*. In 1975 she was bought by Carnival and renamed *Carnivale*. She became the *Fiesta Marina* in 1993, *Olympic* in 1994 and *The Topaz* in 1998.

Kungsholm, Empress of Canada, Ben My Chree (1966/2,762grt) and the *Queen Of The Isles* (1965/515grt) berthed at Princes Landing Stage.

Windsor Castle, 1960, Union Castle Line, 37,640grt, 239m x 28m, 22 ½ knots. Built by Cammell Laird at Birkenhead, she sailed on her maiden voyage on 18 August 1960 from Southampton to Cape Town and Durban. She completed the final passenger sailing by the Union Castle Line in August 1977. She was sold to John Latsis of Piraeus in 1977 and renamed *Margarita L*. She is presently laid up in Greece.

Caronia, 1949, Cunard Line, 34,274grt, 218m x 28m, 22 knots. She sailed on her maiden voyage from Southampton to New York on 4. January 1949 and, due to her distinctive colour scheme, she soon became known as the 'Green Goddess'. *Caronia* completed many world cruises during her career with Cunard Line. In 1967 she was laid up at Southampton. She was then sold to Universal Line and renamed *Columbia*, followed by *Caribia* in 1968. While cruising in 1969, she suffered an engine room explosion and was towed to New York where she was laid up. In 1974 she was sold to the breakers in Taiwan and was driven ashore on Guam in the Pacific Ocean where she was broken up.

Two

Cargo Vessels

Alfred Holt, Ellennan, Cunard and Clan Line were the major providers of international freight services from the Port of Liverpool. Shippers could arrange for goods to be transported to any port of the globe by steamer from the Mersey. Cargo vessels would unload in Liverpool Docks, and some would then move over to the Birkenhead Dock system to load cargoes for India, the Far East, Africa and South America.

Most of the main shipping lines had their own loading berths, providing a regular weekly or monthly service to their customers. Berths were rarely empty: when one vessel sailed, another arrived to commence loading. Cunard used berths at Huskisson Dock, Clan Line and Alfred Holt used Vittoria Dock, Birkenhead, while Ellerman and Hall Lines had berths in the West Float.

The Tranmere Oil Terminal was built to allow large tankers to discharge crude oil destined for the Stanlow Oil Terminal, seventeen miles away, at Ellesmere Port in Cheshire. In 1970, this facility was used by 225 vessels, which discharged 11,123,280 tons of oil. Iron-ore was shipped through a specialized terminal at Bidston Dock, loaded onto rail wagons, and trans-shipped to the John Summers Iron Works in North Wales.

In the 1960s it became apparent that cargo shipped in containers would rationalize the shipping industry, prompting the Mersey Docks and Harbour Company to build a special container terminal at Seaforth.

MacAndrew Line's *Villegas* (1955/1,216grt) approaches Langton Dock at the end of a voyage from Spain.

Mentor (1945/7,642grt) berths opposite *Elpenor* (1954/7,757grt) in the Birkenhead Dock system. *Mentor* was broken up in Split in 1971 and *Elpenor* in Kaohsiung in 1979.

The Rea tug *Grassgarth* (1953/231grt) assists the Blue Funnel liner *Clytoneus* (1948/8,214grt) into her berth in Gladstone Dock. *Clytoneus* was transferred to the Elder Dempster Line service in 1971 and, later that year, was sold to the breakers in Kaohsiung.

Cunard Freight Service

Cunard R.M.S. "Queen Elizabeth," World's Largest Liner

Liverpool to New York

Cunard Freight Services sailing notice No.65 listing sailings to New York, Montreal and Gulf Ports, for October and November 1964.

A Bank Line vessel berths in Gladstone Dock to await a drydock following serious collision damage to her bow.

Tantalus, 1945, Blue Funnel Line, 7,713grt, 139m x 19m, 16 knots. Built as *Macmurray Victory*, she was renamed *Polyphemus* in 1946. In 1960 she became *Tantalus* and in 1969 she was once agian renamed to become *Pelops*. She was finally broken up later that year.

A bulk carrier docks at Cavendish Quay, in the West Float in Birkenhead. Berthed ahead of her is the Mersey Dock's heavy lift crane *Mammoth*.

Cargo for Hong Kong and Japan is loaded on to the *Peleus* (1949/10,093grt) at the Blue Funnel Line berth, at Vittoria Dock, Birkenhead.

Devon City (1960/10,300grt) berths at Birkenhead, in Alfred Dock. She was sold by her owners, Reardon Smith & Co., in 1972 and renamed *Executive Venture*. In 1974 she became the *Tong Beng*, in 1978 the *Pentay* and, in 1986, she was finally broken up.

Ships of the Blue Funnel, Ellerman and Harrison Lines are docked together on the morning tide at Alfred Dock, Birkenhead, awaiting towage to their loading berths in Vittoria Dock and the West Float.

Clan Brodie (1940/7,473grt) loading cargo for India at Vittoria Dock, Birkenhead. She was completed as HMS *Athene*, and transported forty aircraft during the Second World War. Returned to the Clan Line in 1946, she was broken up in Hong Kong in 1963.

Clan Matheson, 1957, Clan Line, 7,685grt, 153m x 20m, 16 knots. Broken up in Kaohsiung in 1978.

Clan Macintosh, 1951, Clan Line, 6,487grt, 144m x 19m, 15 knots. Named *Sanil* in 1978 and broken up in 1980.

Clan Ross, 1966, Clan Line, 10,542grt, 161m x 21m, 17 $\frac{1}{2}$ knots. Named *Kinpurnie Castle* in 1976, *Kinpurnie Universal* in 1979 and *Syros Reefer* in 1982. Broken up in 1984.

Linguist, 1947, Harrison Line, 6,736grt, 141m x 17m, 14 knots. Named *Jade Venture* in 1966. Broken up at Kaohsiung in 1969.

Author, 1959, Harrison Line, 8,715grt, 149m x 18m, 15 knots. She became *Humber* of Stena Atlantic Line in 1978 and was broken up at Gadani beach in 1979.

Crofter, 1951, Harrison Line, 8,377grt, 143m x 18m, 12 knots. Sold to Greece and renamed *Aghios Georgios* in 1971. In 1976 another renaming saw her become *San Georgio II*. In 1977 she was broken up in Spain.

Factor, 1948. Harrison Line, 6,533grt, 141m x 17m, 14 knots. Loading cargo for Barbados, Trinidad, Curacoa and Maracaibo on a joint service to Venezuela with the Compania Anonima Venezolana de Navigacion. She was broken up in 1972 in Bilbao, Spain.

Inventor, 1964, Harrison Line,
9,171grt, 150m x 19m, 17 knots.
Renamed *Penta World* in 1981 and
broken up 1985 in Kaohsiung, after
being laid up at Singapore since
1982.

Governor, 1952, Harrison Line,
8,202grt, 141m x 18m, 13 knots
In 1972 she became the *Diamondo*,
for Pleiades Shipping Co. and was
broken up in 1979, in Spain, after
being laid up for two years.

City of Lancaster (1958/4,949grt) and *City of Eastbourne* (1962/10,000grt) pass in the River Mersey. *City of Lancaster* was sold in 1979 and renamed *Lancaster*. Following a collision in the Irish Sea in 1979, she was eventually sold for scrap in 1982. *City of Eastbourne* was renamed *City of Toronto* in 1971. She became the *Kota Cantik* in 1978 and was broken up in 1984.

City of Liverpool (1949/7,612grt) and *City of Lichfield* (1961/4,976grt) anchored in the river, prior to entering the Birkenhead dock system.

City of Bedford, 1950, Ellerman Lines, 7,341grt, 148m x 19m, 14 knots. Broken up in Spain in 1972.

City of Philadelphia, 1949, Ellerman Lines, 7,591grt, 148m x 19m, 15 knots. Named *Kaptaspyro* in 1967, renamed *Spyro* in 1970 and broken up one year later.

City of New York, (1947/8,420grt) and *City of Pretoria* (1947/8,450grt) berthing at Alfred Dock, Birkenhead.

City of Dundee, 1961, Ellerman Lines, 4,964grt, 132m x 18m, 15 knots. Broken up in 1984.

Palmelian, 1948, Ellerman & Papayanni
Line, 1,533grt, 83m x 13m, 12 knots.
Broken up in Spain in 1970.

Crosbian, 1947, Ellerman &
Papayanni Line, 1,518grt, 83m x
13m, 12 knots. Renamed Mabuhay
in 1967. She was eventually broken
up in 1980.

Orcoma, 1966, Pacific Steam Navigation Co., 10,300grt, 155m x 21m, 18 knots. She was built for the Nile Shipping Company and chartered to P.S.N.C. for a twenty year period. In 1970 she was sold to an Indonesian company and renamed *Ek Daya Samudera*. She was broken up in Kaohsiung in 1984.

Carnatic (1956/11,144grt), *Pizarro* (1955/8,564grt) and *Cienfuegos* (1959/5,407grt) berthed in Canada Dock, Liverpool in 1966.

Cuzco, 1951, Pacific Steam Navigation Co., 8,038grt, 153m x 20m, 15½ knots. Reamed *Benattow* in 1965, she was then broken up at Kaohsiung in 1977.

Durango, 1944, Royal Mail Line, 9,801grt, 143m x 20m, 15 knots. Renamed *Ruthenic* in 1966, *Sussex* in 1967, she was broken up in 1968.

Yoma, 1958, Henderson Line, 6,301grt, 140m x 19m, 14 knots. Built as *Daru*, she was renamed *Yoma* in 1965 and reverted to her original name in 1966. In 1979 she renamed *Lone Eagle* and *Anjo One* in 1980. She was then broken up in 1982.

Adelaide Star, 1950, Blue Star Line, 12,964grt, 175m x 22m, 18 knots. Loading cargo for the north Pacific ports of Los Angeles, San Francisco, Oakland, Seattle, Portland and Vancouver. She sustained engine damage on a voyage from Timaru to Liverpool on 8 March 1975 and was sold to Far Eastern shipbreakers at Pusan.

Australia Star, 1965, Blue Star Line, 10,915grt, 160m x 21m, 20 knots. Named *Concordia Gulf* in 1972, *Cortina* in 1974, *Candy Ace* in 1985, she was and dismantled later that year.

South Africa Star, 1944, Blue Star Line, 8,529grt, 150m x 21m, 16 knots. She was built as the *Winjah* for the United States Navy as an escort carrier, and transferred to the Royal Navy in 1945 as HMS *Reaper*. She was transferred back to the US Navy at the end of the war. Acquired by Blue Star she was renamed in 1948 and was converted to a heavy-lift ship in 1962. She was sold to the breakers in 1967 but was resold to C.Y. Tung's Orient Overseas Line for whom she traded until finally scrapped in 1972 in Taiwan. C.Y. Tung was one of the Far East's largest ship owners and purchased Cunard's *Queen Elizabeth* to convert into a floating university and school ship.

Runswick, 1956, Headlam & Son, 6,229grt, 145m x 19m, 14 knots. Named *Margaret H* in 1973, *Osia Irini Chrysovalandou III* in 1977 and broken up in 1982.

Brescia, 1945, Cunard Line, 3,817grt, 103m x 15m, 11 ½ knots. Built as *Hickory Isle*, she was renamed *Brescia* in 1947, *Timber One* in 1966 and *Deepsea Miner* in 1970. She was eventually broken up in 1974.

Saxonia (1964/5,586grt), *Ivernia* (1964/5,586 grt), *Scythia* (1964/5,837grt) and *Sylvania* (1957/21,989grt) berthed together in Huskisson Dock, Liverpool.

Port Nicholson, 1962, Port Line, 11,711grt, 175m x 23m, 18 knots. Broken up in Kaohsiung in 1979.

Port Lyttleton, 1947, Port Line, 7,413grt, 149m x 20m, 15 knots. Broken up at Faslane by Shipbreaking Industries Ltd in 1972.

Port Chalmers, 1933, Port Line, 8,719grt, 155m x 20m, 15 ½ knots. In 1941 and 1942 she took part in the relief of Malta, when many merchant vessels were sunk despite the heavy naval escort which included the battleship HMS *Nelson* and the carrier HMS *Ark Royal*. She was the only merchant vessel that was undamaged and was finally scrapped in 1965.

Port Auckland, 1949, Port Line, 11,945grt, 171m x 21m, 17 knots. In 1976 *Port Auckland* was sold to Gulf Fisheries Kuwait and renamed *Mashaallah*. She was converted to a sheep carrier and used for the Middle East to Australia trade. This continued until 1979 when, following engine breakdowns, she was sold for scrapping at Kaohsiung.

Cymric, 1953, Shaw Savill Line, 11,182grt, 156m x 21m, 17 knots. Renamed *Durango* in 1973, she was broken up in 1975. The original Shaw Savill company was founded by Robert Shaw and Walter Savill in 1858. Steam was introduced to the company when it hired surplus White Star liners in the early 1880s for the New Zealand trade. The tradition of naming ships with an 'ic' at the end dated from this time.

Ionic, 1959, Shaw Savill Line, 10,978grt, 156m x 21m, 17 knots. Sailing under the Dolphin Line service to Fremantle, Melbourne, Sydney and Townsville, the *Ionic* arrives in the Mersey in November 1969 to load at Gladstone Dock. She was sold in 1978, renamed *Glenparva* and broken up in 1979.

Egton, 1962, Headlam & Son, 7,175grt, 155m x 20m, 14 knots. She was delivered to her owners when freight rates were low and, as a result, spent fourteen months laid up following her trials. In 1967 she ran aground off Whitby and required eighty-seven new shell bottom plates. Following repairs, she undertook various time charters, until she was laid up at Hartlepool on 24 April 1977. She was there for nearly nine years and was sold in 1986 and towed to Finland for demolition.

Merchant Prince, 1950, Prince Line, 3,343grt, 111m x 16m, 13 $\frac{1}{2}$ knots. Built as *Sycamore*, She was renamed *Walsingham* in 1955 and reverted to *Sycamore* in 1957. Renamed *Merchant* in 1965, *Jara*;in 1973, *Meltemi* in 1975, *Temi* in 1977 and *Prince* in 1979. She was broken up later that year.

Warwickshire, 1948, Bibby Line, 8,903grt, 146m x 18m, 15½knots. Warwickshire was sold to the Aegean Steam Navigation Ltd in 1965 and subsequently sold to shipbreakers the following year.

Lancashire, 1963, Bibby Line, 8,919grt, 142m x 20m, 15 knots. She was urchased by Pargola (Shipping) Ltd and resold to the Pan-Islamic Steamship Co. Ltd in 1970. She was then renamed *Safina-E-Haidar* and broken up in 1993.

Manchester Miller, 1959, Manchester Liners, 9,297grt, 143m x 19m, 17 knots. Converted to a container ship in 1970 and renamed *Manchester Quest*. Broken up in Kaohsiung in 1976.

Manchester Shipper, 1943, Manchester Liners, 7,585grt, 141m x 18m, 13 $\frac{1}{2}$ knots. She operated on the Line's services from Manchester to Montreal, Toronto, Detroit and Chicago. Cargo was loaded in Salford Docks and then the vessel proceeded down the Manchester Ship Canal to Eastham and into the River Mersey. She was broken up in 1969.

Maskeliya, 1954, Brocklebank Line, 7,350grt, 144m x 18m, 15 knots. Employed in owner's services to Jeddah, Aden, Djibouti, Maldives, Colombo, Madras and Calcutta, until she was sold in 1969 to become the *Ocean Joy*. She was broken up in Taiwan in 1972.

Markhor, 1963, Brocklebank Line, 6,867grt, 147m x 20m, 16 $\frac{1}{2}$ knots. Renamed in 1982 as the *Kara Unicorn*, she was broken up in China in 1984 after twenty-one years' service.

Africa Palm, 1953, Palm Line, 5,410grt, 138m x 18m, 10½ knots. Sold to Gulf Shipping Line in 1972 and renamed *Savoydean*. She caught fire at Calcutta on 24 July 1975, was declared a total loss by underwriters and broken up.

Warkworth, 1962, R.S. Dalgliesh Ltd, 9,721grt, 151m x 19m, 13 knots. She was employed in general charter work for her owners but was sold in 1970 to become the *Salamat*. In 1974 she was sold and renamed *Philippa*. She changed owners again that year when she was bought by a Greek company, Ultramar Belgrano S.A. On 9 January 1981 she was seriously damaged by shellfire at Fao, Iraq, and declared a total loss.

Limerick, 1952, Avenue Shipping Co, 6,443grt, 140m x 18m, 14 knots. Built as *Enton*; renamed *Limerick* in 1955, *Howra* in 1970 and *Golden Haven*in 1972. Broken up in Karachi in 1982.

Devon, 1946, Federal Steam Navigation Co., 9,940grt, 151m x 20m, 16 knots. Broken up at Hong Kong in 1971.

Benreoch, 1952, Ben Line, 10,142grt, 154m x 20m, 17 knots. Renamed *Tudis* in 1976 and broken up three years later in 1979.

Benmacdhui, 1948, Ben Line, 7,847grt, 145m x 18m, 15 knots. Spent all of her career under Ben Line ownership until she was sold to shipbreakers in Dalmuir, where she arrived on 23 April 1972.

Woodarra, 1957, British India Line, 8,753grt, 159m x 21m, 17½ knots. Renamed *Pando Gulf*; in 1968 and *Benalbanach* in 1974, she was then broken up in 1978.

Fair Head, 1957, G. Heyn & Sons, 1,573grt, 79m x 13m, 13½ knots. Renamed *Maldive Sea* in 1973. She was broken up in 1983.

Tewkesbury, 1959, Houlder Bros, 8,532grt, 139m x 19m, 13 ½ knots. Lineas Maritimas Argentinas, Lamport & Holt and Houlder Brothers ran a joint River Plate service from Liverpool, Swansea, Newport and Glasgow to Montevideo, Buenos Aires and Rosario loading at Alexandra Dock. *Tewkesbury* was sold in 1973 and renamed *Caminito*. In 1982 she was again renamed and called *Brazil*. A year later she was broken up.

Swan River, 1959, Houlder Bros, 9,637grt, 148m x 20m, 13½knots. Renamed *Premier Atlantic* in 1971, *Confidence Express* in 1973, *Bachlong* in 1979 and *Eastern Concord* in 1980. She was eventually broken up in 1983.

Tangistan, 1950, Strick Line, 7,383grt, 146m x 18m, 12½knots. She operated for the joint Strick & Ellerman Line service to Kuwait, Bandar Shahpour, Khorramshahr and Basrah which normally loaded at South East No.3 Canada Dock. Broken up in 1972.

Shahristan, 1965, Strick Line, 9,280grt, 153m x 21m, 16 knots. Renamed *Strathappin* in 1975, *Irenes Ideal* in 1979 and *Ideal* in 1982, she was then broken up in 1985.

Oakbank, 1963, Bank Line, 6,167grt, 148m x 19m, 15 knots. Renamed *Good Spirit* in 1978, *Discovery* in 1984 and broken up in 1985.

Nessbank, 1953, Bank Line, 5,690grt, 137m x 18m, 14 knots. Renamed *Paris* in 1973 and *Tithis* in 1978. Broken up in 1981.

Beaverpine, 1962, Canadian Pacific, 4,514grt, 113m x 16m, 15 knots. Renamed *CP Explorer* in 1971, *Moira* in 1973, and *Trade Container* in 1981. Broken up in 1986.

Polydora, (1949/2,755grt) completed thirty-one voyages on charter to the Canadian Pacific Line between 1964 and 1969. Shown at their loading berth at North No.1 Gladstone Dock in June 1969.

Geestcape, 1966, Geest Industries, 7,679grt, 149m x 19m, 21 knots. Anchored in the Mersey in 1966, prior to docking at high water. She normally operated to Grenada, St Vincent, St Lucia and Barbados. She became the *Nyombe* in 1975 and was broken up in 1982.

Hereford Beacon, 1955, Phs. Van Ommeren, 9,505grt, 158m x 18m, 12 knots. Renamed *Scherpendrecht* in 1968, *Nike* in 1970 and *Eastern Unity* in 1976. Broken up in 1979.

Longstone, 1960, Bamburgh Shipping, 13,062grt, 160m x 21m, 12 knots. Renamed *Parnassos* in 1977 and *Amesia Tria* in 1985, she was then broken up in 1985.

Silversand, 1958, Silver Line, 10,887grt, 153m x 21m, 13 knots. Renamed *Alecos* in 1973 and broken up in 1982.

Eugene Lykes, 1945, Lykes Bros, 8,191grt, 140m x 19m, 15½ knots. Renamed *Ocean Express* and broken up in 1970 after a long, useful life.

American Packer, 1943, United States Lines, 8,315grt, 140m x 19m, 16 knots. Built as *Titan*, she was renamed *American Packer* in 1968 and broken up in 1970.

The Presdente Kennedy, (1965/9,084grt) berthed in Bidston Dock in Birkenhead. She was owned by Cia. De Navigation Lloyd Brasueiro and was loading cargo for a voyage to South American ports.

Johnson Line's *Los Angeles* (1948/7,216grt) and the Blue Funnel liner *Patroclus* (1950/10,109grt) discharging cargo at Alexandra Dock. *Los Angeles* was broken up in Spain in 1972.

Rio Dulce, 1966, Empresa Lineas Maritimas Argentinas S.A., 5,904grt, 150m x 19m, 19 knots. Broken up in 1984.

Rikke Skou, 1955, Ove Skou Line, 4,220 grt, 127m x 18m, $17\frac{1}{2}$ knots. Renamed *Lady Vivian* in1969 and *Falcon Friendship* in 1975. Broken up in 1979.

Ahmado Bello (1963/6,127grt) of the Nigerian National Line loads cargo from barges in the South Dock's system. She was sold in 1981 and renamed *Ronson*. Renamed *Ionian Dream* in 1985, she was broken up at Gadani Beach, in Pakistan, later that year.

Titov Veles, 2,324grt, was built in 1962 as the *Tercia*. She became the *Titov Veles* in 1966 and renamed the *Haidera* in 1981. Subsequently sold to the breakers in 1983.

South African Shipper, 1954, Safmarine Ltd, 7,898grt, 153m x 20m, 17 knots. Built as *Clan Robertson*. Renamed *Umzinto* in 1959, *Rooibok* in 1960, *South African Shipper* in 1961 and *S.A.Shipper* in 1966. Broken up in 1975.

South African Victory, 1945, Safmarine Ltd, 7,605grt, 139m x 19m, 15 knots. Names; b. *Westbrook Victory*; 1947, *Vegelegen*; 1961, *South African Victory*; 1966, *S.A.Victory*; broken up in 1969.

Safforo Maru, 1961, NYK Line, 9,605grt, 155m x 20m, 18 knots. Broken up in 1980.

Kii Maru, 1966, NYK Line, 11,931grt, 171m x 23m, 21 knots. Once a regular visitor to the Mersey, *Kii Maru* is shown here arriving at Birkenhead to load at Mortar Mill Quay for Hong Kong, Kobe, Nagoya and Yokohama. She was broken up in 1985.

Indian Resource, 1956, India Steamship Co. Ltd, 7,391grt, 163m x 19m, 17½ knots. The India Steamship Company ran regular sailings from European ports, as well as London, South Wales and Liverpool to Port Said, Aden, India and Pakistan. *Indian Resource* was sold to the shipbreakers in Bombay where she arrived on 3 August 1978.

Rupsa, 1958, National Shipping Corporation of Pakistan, 8,525grt, 145m x 19m, 14 knots. Built as *Montcalm*, she was renamed *La Falda* in 1958, *Rupsa* in 1964 and *Caron P.E.* in 1978. She was eventually broken up in 1980.

Sarfaraz Rafiqi, 1966, National Shipping Corporation of Pakistan, 7,236grt, 152m x 20m, 18 knots. Broken up in 1987.

Bagh-E-Karachi, 1964, Pakistan National Shipping Line, 8,999grt, 155m x 20m, 17 knots. Broken up in 1985.

Three

Coastal Vessels

Liverpool was the main port for passenger traffic to the Republic of Ireland, Northern Ireland and the Isle of Man. There was a nightly service to Dublin and Belfast from Princes Dock and a daily service to Douglas, Isle of Man, on the steamers of the Isle of Man Steam Packet.

Birkenhead Docks provided winter lay-up berths for the 'Isle of Man boats', with up to six berthed at Morpeth Dock from September to April.

Passenger and freight services were provided by the main coastal shipping lines, as well as by other smaller companies, many of whom were based locally with their ships registered in the Port of Liverpool.

Although the Irish trade provided the majority of coastal cargo through the port, services to other European destinations were also available. Ellennan and Papayanni sailed to Portugal, Spain and other Mediterranean ports; Metric Line sailed to Belgium and Holland, and Moss Hutchinson served Greece, Lebanon and Turkey.

Meath (1960/1,558grt), *Munster* (1948/4,142grt) and *Leinster* (1948/4,115grt) load cargo at the British & Irish Line berth at Princes Dock, Liverpool.

Details of Day Excursions from Liverpool to Llandudno, provided by the Isle of Man Steam Packet in 1971, showing prices in decimal and pre-decimal curency.

Ulster Prince (1937/4,303grt) at Princes Landing Stage preparing to take a daylight sailing to Belfast. These sailings were unusual, as the 'Belfast boats' normally sailed from both ports overnight.

Belfast Steamship Company *Ulster Queen* (1967/4,270grt) is seen here loading vehicles and passengers at South West Princes Dock prior to her maiden voyage on 6 June 1967.

Cammell Laird, 1936, Cammell Laird Ltd, 3,290grt, 104m x 15m, 17 knots. Built as *Royal Ulsterman*, she became *Cammel Laird* in 1968, *Sounion* in 1970 and was broken up in 1973.

Scottish Coast, 1957, Burns & Laird Lines, 3,817grt, 105m x 16m, 17 knots. Renamed *Galaxias* in 1968 and *Princesa Amorosa* in 1989.

Irish Coast, 1952, Coast Lines, 3,824grt, 104m x 16m, 17½ knots. Renamed *Orpheus* in 1968 and *Semiramis II*, *Achilleus* and *Apollon II* in 1969, she then became *Regency* in 1981. Broken up in 1989. Coast Lines was a subsidiary company of Burns & Laird.

Ulster Monarch, 1929, Belfast Steamship Co., 3,815grt, 109m x 14m, 17 knots. She was broken up in 1966.

A view from the bridge of the *Ulster Queen* (1967/4,270grt) berthed at the car ferry berth in Princes Dock, showing the Royal Liver Building and Pier Head in the background.

Birkenhead & Wallasey Corporation ferries berth at the Pier Head, prior to its redevelopment and the building of a new bus terminal, restaurant and shops.

Ulster Queen, 1967, Belfast Steamship Co., 4,270grt, 115m x 16m, 17½ knots. Renamed *Med Sea* in 1982, *Al-Eddin* and *Al-Kahera* in 1987 and *Poseidonia* in 1988. The *Ulster Queen* and her sister *Ulster Prince* were the first purpose-built car ferries for this service. However, the line was taken over by the P&O Group and both were sold for further trading in 1982.

Ulster Prince, 1967, Belfast Steamship Co., 4,270grt, 115m x 16m, 17½ knots. She was renamed *Lady M* in 1982, *Tangpakorn* in 1985, *Long Hu* in 1987, *Macmosa* in 1988, *Neptunia* in 1994, *Panther* in 1995, *Vatan* in 2000 and *Manar* in 2001.

Leinster, 1948, British & Irish Line, 4,115grt, 112m x 15m, 17½ knots. Renamesd*Leinster I* and *Aphrodite* in 1969. Broken up in 1988.

Munster, 1948, British & Irish Line, 4,142grt, 112m x 15m, 17½ knots. She was renamed three times in 1969: *Munster I, Theseus,* 1969.

Mersey ferry passengers pause to watch the departure of the *Manxman* (1955/2,495grt) on one of her regular sailings to Douglas, Isle of Man.

Meath (1960/1,590grt), *Kilkenny* (1937/1,320grt) and *Munster* (1948/4,142grt) loading cargo in Princes Dock. *Meath* was broken up in 1990 while *Kilkenny* suffered the same fate in 1974, after suffering serious mechanical failure.

Leinster (1968/4,848grt) on a promotional visit to Princes Landing Stage. In 1980 *Leinster* was transferred to the Pembroke Dock for the Cork service and renamed *Innisfallen*.

Munster (1968/4,230grt) moves astern from the car ferry berth and swings in Langton Dock as she leaves on a sailing to Dublin in 1969.

A tranquil scene in Morpeth Dock, Birkenhead, with both Manx and Mersey ferries, as well as smaller sailing vessels laid up for the winter months.

The daily car ferry arrives from the Isle of Man. People wait at the Landing Stage to greet friends or relatives, as the crew secure the vessel and the gangway is lowered.

Koningen Juliana(6,682grt) was built by Cammel Laird in 1968 for the Zeeland Steamship Company's Harwich-Hook of Holland route. She is seen here in the builder's dry dock prior to her leaving for sea trials. She was 131m x 20m and was sold in 1984 and became the *Tromp*. She was resold in 1985 and became the *Moby Prince*. In 1991 she collided with a tanker at Livorno, Italy, causing a fire which killed 143 people on board. The wreck of the vessel was moored at Leghorn and, on 16 May 1998, started to sink. Repairs were carried out and the wreck was towed towed to Aliaga, in Turkey, where it arrived on 22 July 1998 for breaking up.

Ben-My-Chree, 1927, Isle of Man Steam Packet Co., 2,586grt, 112m x 14, 22 $\frac{1}{2}$knots. The '*Ben*' served the Island until 1939, when she became a troop transport. In 1944 she was at Omaha Beach as Headquarters for the 514th Assault Flotilla. She returned to service after the war and was broken up in 1965.

Passengers queue at the gangway to board the day excursion vessel *St Seriol* (1931/1,586grt) for a day trip to Llandudno and Menai Bridge in Angelsey. The vessel was owned by the Liverpool and North Wales Steamship Company which ceased trading in 1961 and *St Seriol* was sold for scrap.

Manxman (1955/2,495) swings in the River Mersey as she prepares to berth at Princes Landing Stage. She passes a Clan Line vessel which is about to dock at Birkenhead.

Monas Isle, 1951, Isle of Man Steam Packet, 2,491grt, 105m x 14m, 21 knots. Broken up in 1980 in Holland.

A bus is loaded onto the foredeck of the Manx steamer *King Orry* (1946/2,485grt) by the Mersey Dock's floating crane for shipment to Douglas, Isle of Man. It was quite common for buses to be carried on the passenger steamers until the introduction of the roll-on/roll-off vessels.

Passengers relax on the stern of the *Snaefel* (1948/2,489grt) as they return from a day excursion to Llandudno in North Wales. Another Isle of Man steamer follows them down the channel into Liverpool.

Tynwald, 1947, Isle of Man Steam Packet, 2,487grt, 105m x 14m, 21 knots. Broken up in 1975 in Spain.

Lady of Mann (1930/3,104grt) in the River Mersey on an early morning departure to the Isle of Man. The '*Lady*' served the Isle of Man Steam Packet for over forty years. She also had a distinguished war career. She was finally broken up in 1971 in Dalmuir.

Monas Isle (1951/2,491grt) receives a coat of paint in drydock at Birkenhead, prior to a summer season in the 1960s.

King Orry, 1946, Isle of Man Steam Packet, 2,485grt, 105m x 14m, 21 knots. She was sold in 1975 but was not broken up until 1979 as she spent some time aground at Glasson Dock. She was finally towed to Queenborough, in Kent, by the tug *Afon Wen* for demolition.

A typical summer Saturday morning at Princes Landing Stage in 1963. *Lady of Mann* (1930/3,104grt) sails for Douglas while passengers board the *Snaefell* (1948/2,489grt) which leaves an hour later.

In 1971 a day excursion to the Isle of Man cost £1.50. Passengers were able to enjoy the sea air, the passing shipping and three to four hours on the island. It was a popular day out and good value for money, especially if the weather was fine and the sea was calm.

Passengers disembark from the *Ben-My-Chree* (1927/2,586grt) at the landing stage, as cars wait to be loaded for the return sailing to the Isle of Man.

On 23 May 1962 the *Manx Maid* (1962/2,724grt) is assisted by tugs in a strong wind, as she leaves on her maiden voyage to Douglas. She was the Isle of Man's first car ferry and survived until 1985 when she was sold. She was broken up at Garston in 1986.

Ben-My-Chree (1966/2,762grt) sails from Liverpool on her maiden voyage, on 12 May 1966. She is saluted by her sister ship *Manx Maid*, which had arrived from Douglas earlier that day. *Ben-My-Chree* was broken up in 1989.

Monas Isle (1951/2,491grt) berths astern of the Cunard liner *Carinthia* (1956/21,947grt) at the end of a sailing from Llandudno.

Tynwald (1947/2,487grt), *Snaefell* (1948/2,489grt) and *Lady of Mann* (1930/3,104grt) coping with the busy Tourist Trophy traffic in early June 1961.

On 15 February 1964 *Monas Isle* went aground on rocks at Peel, Isle of Man. She was towed to Birkenhead and dry-docked for repairs to be completed. The damage was so extensive that a large section of the stern and rudder needed to be replaced and she did not return to service until 14 July that year.

A fine winter's day in 1968 with ships of the Isle of Man Steam Packet and Coast Lines at their winter lay-up berths in Morpeth Dock, Birkenhead.

95

St Andrew, 1932, British Railways, 3,035grt, 100m x 14m, 21 knots. Broken up in 1967.

Duke of Rothesay, 1957, British Railways, 4,780grt, 114m x 17m, 21 knots. Broken up in 1975.

Stella Marina (1965/1,588grt) berthed at Cavendish Quay, on the West Float in Birkenhead. Shortly after this photograph was taken, in March 1969, she reopened a service from Fleetwood to Douglas.

Queen of the Isles, 1965, Isles of Scilly Steamship Co. Ltd, 515grt, 48m x 9m, 13 knots. Renamed *Olovaha* in 1972, *Gulf Explorer* in 1982, *Queen of the Isles* in 1987, *Island Princess* in 1972, and *Western Queen* in 1996. She was beached at Ranadi after Cyclone Justin in 1997.

Viking II, 1964, Otto Thoresen, 3,608grt, 99m x 18m, 19½knots. Renamed *Earl William* in 1977, *Pearl William* in 1992, *Mar Julia* in 1996, *Cesme Stern* in 1998 and *Windward 11* in 2001. This photograph was taken in 1964 when the owner of the vessel took her to a number of major British ports to promote his new service from Southampton to France.

Bardic Ferry, 1957, Atlantic Steam Navigation Co. Ltd, 2,550grt, 103m x 16m, 14 knots. Renamed *Nasim II* in 1976 and broken up in 1988. Several of the Atlantic Steam vessels operated from the Port of Preston across the Irish Sea. They often came to Liverpool for their annual winter overhaul.

St Trillo, 1936, Liverpool & North Wales Steamship Co., 314 grt, 48m x 8m, 13½ knots. Built as *St Silio*, she was renamed *St Trillo* in 1945. Converted to a floating restaurant in 1972, she was broken up the same year. *St Trillo* normally operated on short cruises from Llandudno in North Wales to Anglesey. She is seen here on a charter to the Mersey Docks & Harbour Board promoting the Port of Liverpool to its customers.

A view of Cammell Laird's fitting out basin in 1966 showing a Blue Star Line cargo vessel and Belfast Steamship Companies car ferry *Ulster Queen* (1967/4,270grt) nearing completion.

Kingsnorth Fisher, 1966, James Fisher & Sons, 2,480grt, 84m x 17m, 12 knots. Renamed *New Generation* in 1990 and *New Gen* in 2001. She arrived at Alang on 19 December 2001 to be broken up.

Spaniel, 1955, Coast Lines, 891grt, 68m x 12m, 11 knots. Built as *Brentfield*, she was renamed *Spaniel* in 1959 and *Conister* in 1973. She was then broken up in 1981.

Buffalo, 1961, Link Lines, 2,163grt, 79m x 13m, 12 knots. Renamed *Norbrae* in 1972, *Roe Deer* in 1974, *Newfoundland Container* in 1977, *Caribbean Victory* in 1985, *Lefkimmi* in 1986, *St George* in 1988, and *Container Express* in 1992. She was abandoned in 1993.

Lancashire Coast, 1954, Coast Lines, 1,283grt, 78m x 12m, 12 knots. Renamed *Trojan Prince* in 1968, *Lancashire Coast* in 1969, reverted to *Lancashire Coast* in 1969 and renamed *Paolino* in 1980. She was eventually broken up in 1984.

Ulster Sportsman, 1936, Belfast Steamship Co., 789grt, 72m x 11m, 13 ½ knots. Built as *Lairdswood*, renamed *Ulster Sportsman* in 1959, *Trnsrodopi II* in 1966 and *Alnilam* in 1968. She was broken up in 1970

Wirral Coast, 1962, Coast Lines, 881grt, 62m x 11m, 12 knots. Renamed *Shevrell* in 1972; *Portmarnock* in 1974; and *Nadia I* in 1979. She sank in 1985.

Mersey Coast, 1938, Coast Lines, 509grt, 62m x 10m, 10 knots. Sold and renamed *Agios Artemios* in 1969. Two years later, in 1971, she was abandoned.

Ulster Weaver, 1946, Belfast Steamshisp Co., 498grt, 61m x 9m, 12 knots. Built as *Ulster Duchess*; renamed *Jersey Coast* in 1946, *Ulster Weaver* in 1954, *Kentish Coast* in 1964 and *Salmiah Coast* in 1968.

Hibernian Coast, 1947, Coast Lines, 1,258grt, 84m x 12m, 14 knots. Renamed in 1968 as *Port Said Coast* and broken up in 1975.

Pacific Coast, 1947, Coast Lines, 1,188grt, 81m x 12m, 12 knots. Renamed *Kuwait Coast* in 1968, *Mohamed Nassar* in 1974 and *Nassar* in 1975. She was abandoned during a gale at Port Rashid on 29 November 1976, refloated in 1977 and was deliberately sunk off a breakwater in shallow water.

Tuskar, 1962, Clyde Shipping Co., 1,115grt, 83m x 13m, 14 knots. She was delivered in June 1962 for the Liverpool-Waterford route. In 1968 she was sold to Losinjska Plovidba Oour Brodarstro and for twenty years was employed as a livestock carrier called the *Brioni*. In 1988 she was sold to the breakers.

Empire Nordic, 1945, Atlantic Steam Navigation Co., 4,157grt, 106m x 16m, 10 knots. Built as LST 3026. Renamed *Charger* in 1946 and *Empire Nordic* in 1955. Broken up in 1968.

A Victorian warehouse is demolished to enable land to be available for a car storage area at Princes Dock. This was just one of many projects that were undertaken in the 1960s to improve facilities on the dock estate.

The ship-repair industry was dominated by Cammell Laird, Grayson Rollo & Clover and Harland & Wolff. They were all responsible for major and minor projects on vessels needing repair or structural damage. Here a group of workers carry out repairs to the *Lancashire Coast* following a collision.

Four
Mersey Ferries

Benedictine monks were recorded as operating a ferry service across the River Mersey in the twelfth century, and a Royal Decree confirmed their right to maintain a service to Liverpool.

The Mersey Ferries now operate services from Liverpool to Birkenhead and Wallasey, but in the past the Wallasey and Birkenhead Corporation operated services to New Brighton, Egremont and Eastham. The present fleet was originally built for the Birkenhead Corporation and was transferred to the ownership of the Mersey Ferries following local government reorganisation in the 1970s.

The ferries play a vital role in the local transport infrastructure, and offer a valuable leisure resource for the people of Merseyside and visitors to the region. They provide a unique service by enabling people to sail on a famous river which has a long and distinguished past.

Wallasey Corporation Ferries *Leasowe* (1951/567grt) and *Egremont* (1952/566grt) arrive at the Princes Landing Stage from Seacombe and New Brighton.

Royal Iris, 1951, Wallasey Corporation, 1,234grt, 49m x 15m, 12 knots. Sold for use as a restaurant ship in 1994, she moved to Cardiff in 1995 and to London in 1998.

Wallasey, 1927, Wallasey Corporation, 606grt, 46m x 15m, 12 knots. This photograph was taken in January 1964, just before she was sold to shipbreakers in Belgium.

Royal Daffodil, 1958, Wallasey Corporation, 609grt, 48m x 15m, 12 knots. Built as *Royal Daffodil II*, renamed *Royal Daffodil* in 1968, *Ioulis Keas II* in 1978 and *Agia Kyriaki* in 1990.

Mountwood, 1960, Birkenhead Corporation, 464grt, 46m x 12m, 12 knots. A member of the present fleet, she was renamed *Royal Iris of the Mersey* in 2002.

Overchurch, 1962, Birkenhead Corporation, 468grt, 47m x 12m, 12 knots. Renamed in 1999 as *Royal Daffodil* and still a member of the present fleet.

Woodchurch, 1960, Birkenhead Corporation, 464grt, 46m x 12m, 12 knots. A current Birkenhead ferry.

Egremont, 1952, Wallasey Corporation, 566grt, 45m x 10m, 12 knots. Sold to the Island Cruising Club, Salcombe, Devon, in 1976, she retained the name *Egremont*. She was drydocked and overhauled at Penzance, Cornwall in November 2002.

Leasowe, 1951, Wallasey Corporation, 567grt, 45m x 10m, 12 knots. Sold and renamed in 1974 as *Naias II*. In 1980 she was renamed again as *Cavo Doro*.

Five
Tugs and other Small Vessels

Towage vessels and other smaller ships provide a vital service for the efficient organisation of any major port operation. Tugs enable vessels to dock and undock safely at all tides and in all types of weather, bunker barges provide fuel and oil to the ships, and coastal barges trans-ship cargo from smaller ports in the area. Without these little ships the port would be unable to function and the safety of all port users would be reduced. In Liverpool, the Port Authority was responsible for providing pilotage services, dredging all of the docks and main shipping channels, and operating a number of heavy-lift floating cranes such as the 'Mammoth', capable of lifting up to 200 tons.

The Mersey Docks and Harbour Company was also responsible for the production of charts of Liverpool Bay and approaches to river entrances. To enable them to carry out these duties they operated a fleet of small survey craft equipped with appropriate equipment, such as echo sounding devices.

The removal of wrecks and recovery of shipping casualties, such as those resulting from collisions, was dealt with by the provision of two salvage vessels equipped to deal with emergencies. They carried fire-fighting and cutting equipment, using their fifteen ton capacity derricks.

The Rea Towing Company's vessel *Rosegarth* (1954/255grt) pictured in the Mersey off Langton Dock. Visible are the initial works being carried out at the new Seaforth Dock. *Rosegarth* became the *Afon Wen* in 1970 and the *Pescasseroli* in 1974. She was broken up in 1984.

Alexandra Towing vessels *Canada* (1951/237grt), *Egerton* (1965/142grt) and *Alfred* (1937/215grt) tied up next to a dredger in Brocklebank Dock.

B.C. Lamey (1966/225grt), *J.H.Lamey* (1963/216grt) and *William Lamey* (1959/166grt) were taken over by the Alexandra Towing Company in 1970 and became the *Salthouse*, *Hornby* and *Wapping*.

A photograph taken in the 1960s of various Lamey and Rea tugs 'locking down' in Alfred Dock, Birkenhead prior to a profitable day on the river.

A similar view showing various Lamey and Rea tugs 'locking down'.

Huskisson, 1934, Alexandra Towing Co., 201grt. Broken up in 1965.

Wapping, 1936, Alexandra Towing Co., 201grt. Renamed in 1967 as *Marsh Cock* and broken up in 1968.

Crosby (1937/215grt) and *Brocklebank* (1965/142grt) assist the Cunard liner *Sylvania* (1957/21,989grt) to her berth in Huskisson Dock at the end of a voyage from New York.

North Wall, 1959, Alexandra Towing Co., 219grt. Named *Maestosa* in 1973 and broken up in 1988.

The Alexandra Towing Company was contracted to assist Cunard Line vessels in and out of the Port of Liverpool. Here the *Formby* (1951/237grt) works with two sister-tugs to help the a Cunard liner to her berth in the dock system at Huskisson Dock.

North Buoy, 1959, Alexandra Towing Co., 219 grt. She was sold to Italian owners in 1973 and became the *Caraggioso*. She was sold for breaking up in 1988.

William Lamey, 1959, Lamey Tugs, 166grt. Renamed *Wapping* in 1970 and *Theodoros 1* in 1985.

Edith Lamey, 1942, Lamey Tugs, 147grt. Built as *Robert Hamilton*, renamed C618 in 1959, *Edith Lamey* in 1960, *Martin Oldfield* in 1969 and *Hermes* in 1973. She went to the breakers in 1985.

Black Cock (1939/168grt) helps manoeuvre a Harrison liner into Langton Dock.

Heath Cock (1958/193grt) and *Weather Cock* (1960/165grt). In 1981 both tugs were sold to a Greek company and sank together with the *Canada* off the South Wales coast.

Rea and Cock tugs leave Gladstone River Entrance on their way to various towage duties in the North docks system.

Rossmore (1958/206grt) and *Kilmore* (1958/207grt) were built for the Furness Group to provide towage duties for their vessels in the Port of Liverpool. They were taken over by Rea in 1969 and were renamed *Rossgarth* and *Kilgarth*. *Rossmore* became the *Rozi* in 1981 and was sunk off the coast of Malta in 1992.

Fenella (1951/1,019grt) loading general cargo at the Isle of Man berth at Coburg Dock. She was sold to Cypriot owners in 1973 and renamed *Vasso* M. She caught fire and sank in the Mediterranean in 1978.

A river tug starts its voyage towing barges from the north Liverpool dock system to Eastham and up the Manchester Ship Canal to Salford Docks.

The Shell-Mex and BP oiler *City* berths alongside a Blue Funnel cargo vessel in Alfred Dock, Birkenhead. These small tankers were kept busy servicing all the cargo and passenger ships that used the Port.

Peakdale (1910/507grt) was built as the *Princes Juliana*. She was purchased by Hoveringham Gravels in 1962. She was sold to ship breakers in Dalmuir in 1970.

The Mersey Docks and Harbour Board's floating crane *Mammoth*, (1920/1,524grt) is towed past the Pier Head by tugs of the Alexandra Towing Company. *Mammoth* was sold in 1987.

A heavy lift cargo is loaded on to the *Clan Malcolm* (1957/7,686grt) at the Clan Line berth in Vittoria Dock, Birkenhead. The floating cranes were often seen loading locomotives, carriages or large engineering plant on to vessels bound for Africa, South America and the Far East.

Vigilant, 1953, Mersey Dock & Harbour Board, 728grt, 53m x 11m, 12 $\frac{1}{2}$ knots. Renamed *Staunch* in 1978 and broken up the same year.

Pilot launch *Puffin* berths at Birkenhead docks as *King Orry* (1946/2,485grt) is assisted into Alfred Dock at the end of the summer season in 1971.

The floating crane *Samson* (1960/974grt) lifts a heavy load on to the *Stormont* (1954/906grt) in 1965. *Stormont* was broken up in Tripoli, Lebanon in 1994.

Edmund Gardner, 1953, Mersey Dock & Harbour Board, 617grt, 53m x 10m, 12 knots. Bought by the Merseyside Maritime Museum in 1982.

Aestus (1950/95grt) was owned by the Mersey Docks & Harbour Board and was employed on buoy maintenance and survey work. She was sold to the ship-breakers in 1986.

Portway, 1927, Holms Sand & Gravel Co. Ltd, 298grt, 37m x 7m, 10 knots. Broken up in 1970.